Unusual & Unlucky Deaths in World War One

BEST WISHES,
Darryl Porrino

Darryl Porrino

Copyright © 2017 Darryl Porrino

ISBN-13:978-1979499408

Published by Darryl Porrino

Cover designed by Darryl Porrino

John Robert Sedgwick

Private 2723 & 240755 5th East Lancashire Regiment
Date of death: 25/7/1917

John was born in Padiham, Lancashire in July 1888. He lived with his father John, a cotton weaver, and his mother Nancy Hannah at 5 New Street, Padiham. He had 3 brothers, William, Elisha & Ernest, and 2 sisters, Elizabeth & Rosetta. By 1901 they were living at 14 Kay Street, Padiham. He was a weaver.

John married Mary Elizabeth Ward on the 11th March 1915 and they lived at 81 Shakespeare Street, Padiham. He enlisted in Padiham on the 6th October 1914, into the 5th Battalion East Lancashire Regiment. He died on the 25th July 1917, whilst serving in Egypt.

The circumstances of his death:

Whilst on duty, and whilst sitting on the edge of a railway truck laden with railway locomotive rails, the train ran into a convoy of camels which were being driven by a private. Sedgwick was knocked off the truck and was pinned by the rails, which fell onto him, and rendered him unconscious. He was taken to a dressing station. On the 8th December 1916 he was admitted to the 27th General Hospital at Abbassia, where he was operated on. He was transferred to the 2nd Western General Hospital, Whitworth Street, Manchester, on the 16th July 1917. He was transferred to Didsbury Lodge on the 30th April 1917. He had suffered a fractured spine which resulted in paraplegia. He was discharged on the 14th July 1917 as no longer physically fit for active service. He died of his injuries on the 25th July 1917.

He is buried in Padiham Cemetery.

William Henry Malings

Colour Sergeant 1454 South Lancashire Regiment &
20490 Royal Defence Corps, 306 Protection Company
Date of death: 15/5/1916
Age: 46

William was born in Rhyl in 1869. He lived with his wife Jeanette at 269 Liverpool Road, Warrington, Lancashire. He was a hairdresser. He had previously served with the 8th Battalion South Lancashire Regiment during the Boer war and was awarded the Queen's South Africa Medal with 4 bars and the King's South Africa Medal with 2 bars. He was discharged as medically unfit on the 7th December 1914. He re-enlisted on the 5th June 1915 into the South Lancashire Regiment, and was later transferred to the Royal Defence Corps. He was on duty at an internment camp at Knockaloe, Isle Of Man. He died there on the 15th May 1916.

The circumstances of his death:
The Liverpool Echo 15/7/16:

Manx Murder Charge

At the Court Of Criminal Inquiry, held in Peel, Isle Of Man yesterday, John Williams, of Warrington, sergeant in the Royal Defence Corps, was committed for trial before the Manx Court Of General Gaol Delivery, on a charge of murdering Colour Sergeant William Henry Malings, Royal Defence Corps, also of Warrington, by shooting him with a carbine in the sergeant's quarters, Knockaloe prisoner of war camp on May 15th. The evidence showed that a shot was heard from the quarters, and on entrance being affected, Malings was found shot dead. The only other occupant was Williams, whose recently discharged carbine was on his bed, while a cartridge was missing from his pouch.

The Manchester Evening News reported: 8/8/16

The tragedy which occurred at the Knockaloe Internment Camp, Isle Of Man on May 15th, was recalled at the Court Of General Gaol Delivery held at Douglas, Isle Of Man today, when John Williams, 46 of Warrington, a sergeant in the Royal Defence Corps, was charged with murdering William Henry Malings, Colour Sergeant, Royal Defence Corps. The prisoner, who pleaded not guilty, was defended by Mr Percy Kelly.

The facts of the case, as recounted by the Attorney-General, and proved in evidence, were very remarkable. The prisoner and deceased had been in the sergeant's mess, and so far as could be discovered, there had been no dispute or ill-feeling between them.

About three in the afternoon the prisoner got up and went out. Shortly afterwards Malings also left the mess and Corporal Unsworth saw him going to the sergeant's sleeping quarters. Directly afterwards Unsworth heard a shot fired, and, rushing to the sleeping quarters, found Colour Sergeant Malings lying on his back, a yard or two from the entrance, bleeding from the mouth, nose and ears, and was evidently in a dying condition. The prisoner's rifle was lying on his bed and 2 live cartridges beside it.

Sergeant Stoll asked the prisoner what rifle had done it and the prisoner pointed to his own. On an examination being made, it was found that the prisoner's rifle had been recently used. A clip of 5 cartridges had been removed from his pouch, and 2 live cartridges were found lying on his bed, 2 in his pocket and the 5th was accounted for by the empty case lying on the floor.

Speaking to Sergeant Harrison later, the prisoner said,

"The cur has been the cause of all my troubles since I have been in the Company, and I have made a clean job of it. He is only one of my victims."

Corporal Phillips, who relieved Sergeant Harrison, heard the prisoner mutter to himself, " I am rid of that bastard, I am satisfied."

On being taken into custody by Police Sergeant Urracher, the prisoner said, " I did not give him half enough. I didn't believe in doing things by half."

All the witnesses agreed that the prisoner had a dazed appearance, and in his pocket was found incoherent letters, addressed to his wife at the Shipyard, Warrington.

The Attorney General said that the prisoner, since his arrest, had been medically examined several times, but no signs of insanity had been discovered.

The jury found him guilty whilst insane and the accused was detained.

Walter Ernest Darling Coppin

Private M2/073276 Army Service Corps
 No50 Divisional Supply Column
Date of death: 17/10/1916

Walter was born in Deal, Kent in 1879. He lived with his father Walter & mother Carolina at 13 Water Street, Deal. By 1901 he was a boarder at 64 Claremont Road, Moss Side, Manchester where he was an ironmonger. He married Sarah Smith on the 7th September 1905 and they lived at 64 Darnley Street, Brooks Bar, Manchester.

Walter enlisted in London on the 31st March 1915. He died on the 17th October 1916 at the 21st Field Ambulance. He is buried at Nieppe Communal Cemetery, Pas De Calais, France. II A3.

The circumstances of his death:

Whilst cleaning out Sergeant May's tent with Private M2/073279 John Hiatt, he found a whisky bottle under a table and took a swig. Unfortunately it did not contain whisky but liquid tear gas.

Harry Thomas Page MM

Driver 836613 Royal Field Artillery
Date of death: 26/10/1917
Age: 21

Harry was born in Walsall in 1896. He lived with his father George and mother Sarah at 66 Mount Street, Walsall. He enlisted in Walsall on the 8th December 1915, originally into the 5th South Staffordshire Regiment. He was later transferred to the 1st Warwick Battery Royal Artillery. He was awarded the Military Medal. He was admitted to the No2 Home Counties Field Ambulance on the 21st October 1917 and then to the 27th Field Ambulance on the 26th October 1917 where he died on the same day. He is buried at Saint Julien Dressing Station Cemetery, Langemarck, Belgium.

The circumstances of his death:
Statement from Gunner 164855 T.G. Woods 5/6/18:
" During October I was working on a dug out with 5 other men amongst whom was Gunner Page. The Royal Engineers were working on an old tank some distance away.

There was a large explosion from their direction, and as we saw large masses going up and coming down in our direction, we took cover as was available. Gunner Page, however, was hit by the side door of a tank and was severely wounded. No warning was given to us before the explosion."

Arthur Cecil Rawson

Lance corporal 915 1st Cambridgeshire Regiment
Date of death: 9/8/1914
Age: 25

Arthur was born in Whittlesey, Cambridgeshire in 1888. He lived with his father Charles, a grocery shop owner, and his mother Sarah Jane at 6 Almshouse Street, Whittlesey. He assisted his father in the business. He had a sister, Olive May. He enlisted in Whittlesey. He died on the 9th August 1914. He is buried at Whittlesey Cemetery.

The circumstances of his death:

He was accidentally shot by Private 1547 A Davis who had laid his rifle on his bed on returning from guard duty on the 9th August 1914, and the trigger snagged on a greatcoat button, discharging into Rawson's groin, who was lying on the next bed. He bled to death in minutes.

Private 1547 A Davis was awarded the Distinguished Conduct Medal in 1916 for conspicuous gallantry as a stretcher bearer. He was seriously wounded in the attempt to bring in a wounded man under very heavy fire.

The funeral of Arthur Cecil Rawson.

Septimus Tonge

Major   Machine Gun Corps
Date of death: 9/5/1918
Age: 38

Septimus was born in Pendleton, Manchester in 1880. He lived with his father Robert, and mother Mary at "Lymehurst", Holly Villas, Flixton, Manchester. He had three brothers, Alfred, Rowland & Hargreaves, and two sisters, Mary & Katie.

By 1911 he was living at "Moorside", New Mills, Stockport, where he was now a bank clerk. His father had died in 1909. By the time of his enlistment he was living at "Lymehurst", Roumania Crescent, Llandudno. He enlisted into the Lancashire Fusiliers and was later commissioned into the Machine Gun Corps. He was mentioned in dispatches on the 24th December 1917. He died whilst at home on leave on the 9th May 1918. He is buried at SS Eleri & Mary Churchyard, Llanrhos.

The circumstances of his death:

He had been suffering from shell concussion and depression. He committed suicide.

The Liverpool Daily Echo reported: 11/5/18,

On Thursday Miss Mary Tonge, a sister of the Major, received a letter by the afternoon post, stating that his body could be found in woods near Llandudno. Miss Tonge, with two friends, proceeded to the woods mentioned, and as they approached they heard a shot fired. Proceeding in the direction of the sound they saw Major Tonge lying on the ground, shot through the temple, with a heavy service revolver by his side. He expired almost immediately.

Major Tonge had served in France for 2 years. About six months ago he was sent home suffering from shellshock.

James William Marke

Lance corporal 139705 Royal Engineers
 No3 Depot Company
Date of death: 4/1/1916
Age: 37

James was born in St Giles, London in 1879. He lived with his father James & mother Mary Maria. He later married Louisa. He was a plasterer. He died in Llandudno on the 4th January 1916. He is buried at Great Orme's Head Cemetery, Llandudno.

The circumstances of his death:

The Liverpool Echo reported:
Soldier's Death In Llandudno

This morning a tragic discovery was made at a Llandudno lodging house where soldiers were billeted. One of the soldiers, Lance corporal James Marke, was found with his throat cut. He had almost severed his head from his body. He was attached to the Royal Engineers and belonged to London. He was 37 and had a wife and family.

John Healey

Private 28679 22nd Welsh Regiment
Date of death: 23/11/1915
Age: 25

John was born in Dukinfield, Cheshire on the 22nd September 1890. He lived with his father Edward, a cotton spinner, and his mother Margaret James at 3 Robinson Street, Stalybridge, Cheshire. He was a cotton piecer.

He enlisted in Stalybridge. His Battalion were training at Morfa Camp, Conway, North Wales. He died as a result of drowning in Conway Bay. He is buried at Great Orme's Head Cemetery, Llandudno.

Edward James

Quartermaster Sergeant 52202 Royal Engineers
 6th Depot Company.
Date of death: 3/12/1916
Age: 51

Edward was born in Corey, County Wexford in 1865. By 1911 he was living at 72 York Avenue, Gillingham, Kent, with his wife, Kathleen Helena and their 5 children, John, Norman, Frederick, Eva & Ina. He enlisted into the Royal Engineers on the 18th September 1914. He was attached to the Royal Engineers Training Depot at Deganwy. He was hit by a bus in Deganwy on the 25th November 1915. He died of his injuries on the 3rd December 1916.

John Edward Crellin

Private 28017   4th Royal Lancaster Regiment
Date of death: 21/8/1917

John was born in Manchester in 1894. He lived with his grandparents, John & Ann Crellin at 14 Heath Street, Ancoats, Manchester. He enlisted in Bury, originally into the Lancashire Fusiliers as Private 42070. He was later transferred to the Royal Lancaster Regiment. He died on the 21st August 1917. He is buried at Dozinghem Military Cemetery, West Flanders, Belgium. IV J7.

The circumstances of his death:

He accidentally shot the middle finger off his left hand whilst cleaning his rifle. Whilst being treated at No 61 Casualty Clearing Station a German plane dropped a bomb on the hospital killing him instantly.

Robert Handel Mendelssohn Griffiths

Boy 10623 3rd Border Regiment
Date of death: 29/8/1914
Age: 16

Robert was born in Weymouth, Dorset in 1898. He lived with his father George Pryce, and his mother Lilly at 64 St Leonard's Road, Weymouth. He had a sister Dorothy. By 1911 he was an inmate at The Gordon Boys Home, West End, Cobham, Woking, Surrey. He enlisted in Woking. He died on the 29th August 1914. He is buried at Pembroke Dock Military Cemetery.

The circumstances of his death:

He was killed whilst travelling in a troop train from Pembroke Dock. Another lad, James O'Brien (see next entry) was injured at the same time, and died at Tenby Cottage Hospital 4 days later.

The train passed through Lamphrey Station at a speed of 40mph. There were 4 boys in the compartment and all of them were looking out of the window. Griffiths & O'Brien were struck by the open door of a van which was standing on the siding at the station.

James O'Brien

Boy 10400 3rd Border Regiment
Date of death: 2/9/1914

James was born in Kensington, London. He enlisted in Hounslow. He died as a result of injuries received on the 29th August 1914 (see report above). He is buried at Pembroke Dock Military Cemetery.

Jean Felix Bonnett

Gunner 220326 C Company 103rd Brigade
Royal Field Artillery
Date of death: 11/11/1918
Age: 30

Jean was born in Switzerland in 1888. By 1911 he was living and working at "La Mer Vue" Swiss cafe in Lloyd Street, Llandudno with his boss, Henry Charlier. He was an assistant chocolate maker. He married cafe assistant Lily Mason in 1912. They had 2 children, Jean Louis and Lillian.

He enlisted into the Royal Field Artillery.

Jean died in Italy on the 11th November 1918. He was accidentally killed when he fell from a lorry. He is buried at Giavera British Cemetery, Treviso, Italy. Plot 5, A2.

Cornelius Cafferty MM

Private 24774 Royal Lancaster Regiment
Date of death: 15/1/1919
Age: 30

Cornelius was born in Manchester in July 1888. He lived with his father Cornelius, a gas engine attender, and his mother Mary at 7 Whalley Street, Newton, Miles Platting, Manchester. By 1901 they were living at 33 Vincent Street, Lancaster. He married Eliza Capstick on the 5th April 1913 at St Peter's Church, Lancaster. They lived at 7 Primrose Street, Lancaster. They had a son Leo. He was a master window cleaner.

Cornelius enlisted in Lancaster on the 11th December 1915. He was awarded the Military Medal in the fighting at Givenchy. He died in a flying accident on the 15th January 1919.

The circumstances of his death:

On the 15th January 1919, whilst a patient at Nell Lane Military Hospital, Manchester, he and another private went for a walk to the aerodrome at Alexandra Park. A Captain C.A. Brown was readying a Bristol Fighter for an air test. Cafferty & Davidson persuaded him to take one of them up for a flight. A second person was necessary for this type of plane, a mechanic usually went up. They tossed a coin and Cafferty won. The plane spun in on the turn and nosedived into the ground, bursting into flames on impact. Both bodies were badly charred. A verdict of accidental death was recorded. He is buried in Lancaster Cemetery.

Frederick Woodmore Samuel

Private 4889 8th Royal Scots
Date of death: 29/3/1916
Age: 18

Frederick was born in Dalkeith, Midlothian on the 8th January 1898. His mother was Margaret. He was a forester at Dalkeith Park. He died on the 29th March 1916. He is buried at Chelmsford Cemetery, Essex.

The circumstances of his death:

On the 29th March 1916 he and other men of the Royal Scots went to Chelmsford swimming baths. The others took to the warm pool but Frederick dived into the cold bathes. He was seen to surface but soon sank again. Sergeant Thomas tried to save him but failed due to the cold water. He had drowned but Dr Alford suggested that diving into such cold water may have had an adverse effect on his heart.

Harry Adrian Vaughan

Corporal 74053 6th Signal Company
Royal Engineers
Date of death: 20/5/1917
Age: 28

Harry was born in London in 1889. He lived with his father Charles and mother Sophia at 7a Fontenay Road, Stretham, London. They later moved to 114 High Street, Streatham. He was an automobile designer. He enlisted in Tonbridge Wells on the 26th December 1914. He died on the 20th May 1917.

The circumstances of his death:

Cadet Overbalances & Is Drowned, Plucky Action Commended

Yesterday (Tuesday) afternoon the Cambridge Coroner (Mr H Saunders French) held an inquest at the coroner's court on the body of Cadet Harry Adrian Vaughan, who was drowned in the Granta on Sunday evening. The deceased, along with another cadet, was in a punt, and in turning round he overbalanced and fell into the water. A plucky attempt at rescue was made by another cadet named Harcourt, and after a little time he managed to get the body to land, and artificial respiration was carried out for about 2 hours but with no effect.

Charles Vaughan, 124 High Road, Streatham, London, a mechanical engineer, identified the body as that of his son, who was 28 years of age. Before the war his son was also a mechanical engineer. At the time of his death the deceased was in the Officer Training Cadet Battalion at Trinity College.

Ernest W.H. Lister of the 5th Officer Cadet Battalion, stated that on Sunday evening he and the deceased had engaged a boat at Dolby's and went toward Grantchester. As they were turning around, the deceased, who was punting, lost his balance and fell into the water.

Witnesses shouted for help and a man in uniform, about 25 or 30 yards further down the river, jumped in in full dress. Soon after he shouted that he could not get on because of his heavy boots and witnesses paddled the punt towards him. Then another cadet named Harcourt, came up in a boat and he also jumped in and brought the body on land.

Elijah Cook

Private 43258 8th Worcestershire Regiment
Formerly 58106 Wiltshire Yeomanry
Date of death: 26/11/1918

Elijah was born in Purton, Wiltshire in 1900. He lived with his father Tom and mother Ellen at 63 Green Hill, Lydiard Millicent, Wiltshire. He had 2 brothers, Stanley & Walter. He enlisted in Trowbridge, Wiltshire originally into the Wiltshire Yeomanry. He was later transferred to the Worcestershire Regiment. He died on the 26th November 1918. He is buried at Terlincthun British Cemetery, Wimille, Pas De Calais, France.
The circumstances of his death:

Whilst on a train with his Battlion travelling near Aux-Le-Chateau, the railway engine left the line and the coaches violently collided, one of them being crushed. Four were killed, including Elijah. (See below for the other 3).

Vernon Birch

Private 201334 8th Worcestershire Regiment
Date of death: 26/11/18
Age: 21

Vernon was born in Kidderminster, Worcestershire in 1898. He lived with his mother Harriett at 54 Lea Street, Kidderminster. He had 2 brothers, George & Stanley. They later moved to 75 Offimore Road. He enlisted in Kidderminster. He was killed in the same train crash as Elijah and is buried next to him at Terlincthun British Cemetery.

William Palmer
Private 46090 8th Worcestershire Regiment
Date of death: 26/11/1918

William was born in Birmingham. He enlisted in Birmingham. He died in the same train crash as Elijah Cook. He is buried next to him at Terlincthun British Cemetery.

Leonard Winwood
Private 17912 8th Worcestershire Regiment
Date of death: 26/11/1918

Leonard was born in Upper Arley, Worcestershire in 1892. He lived with his parents William & Susannah. He later married Ada in 1911. They had 3 children, Robert, Wilfred & Marguerite. He enlisted in Worcester. He died in the same train crash as Elijah Cook, Vernon Birch & William Palmer and is buried alongside them at Terlincthun British Cemetery.

Albert Leach

Corporal 305115 15th Tank Corps
Formerley 48657 Manchester Regiment
Date of death: 11/8/1918
Age: 30

Albert was born in Purton, Wiltshire in 1887. He lived with his father Thomas and mother Sarah at 5 Church Street, Purton. He had 5 brothers, Thomas, Henry, James, Arthur and Fred. By 1911 he was a boarder at Red Lodge, Purton, where he was a stable hand. He later married Ruth and they lived at 14 Elmina Road, Swindon.

He enlisted in Manchester, originally into the Manchester Regiment. He was later transferred to the 15th Tank Corps. He died on the 11th August 1918. He is buried at Adelaide Cemetery, Villers-Brettoneux, Somme, France.

The circumstances of his death:

He was run over by his tank.

Joseph Potts

Private 35191 7th Cheshire Regiment
Date of death: 19/7/1916
Age: 18

Joseph lived with his father Joseph, a postman, and his mother Lillian at 1 Court, No1, Off Hibet Road, Macclesfield, Cheshire. He had a brother Reginald. He enlisted in Macclesfield. He died on the 19th July 1916. He is buried at St Leonard's Churchyard, Bedfordshire.

The circumstances of his death:

He was accidentally drowned in a lake at Solihull Training Camp.

Joseph Maher

Private 242130 5th South Lancashire Regiment
Date of death: 15/1/1918
Age: 28

Joseph was born in St Helens, Lancashire in 1890. He lived with his father John and mother Mary at 43 Victoria Street, St Helens. He had 4 brothers, James, Michael, Patrick & John, and a sister Maggie. By 1901 they were living at 13 Fox Street, St Helens. He enlisted in St Helens. He died on the 15th January 1918. He is buried at Bois Guillaume Communal Cemetery, Extension. C 6B.

The circumstances of his death:

He died of acute alcohol poisoning at No8 General Hospital, Rouen.

Hugh James

Private 25695 1st Battalion Royal Welsh Fusiliers
Date of death: 12/6/1918
Age: 39

Hugh was born in Flint in 1880. He lived with his father John, a labourer, and his mother Grace at 19 Commercial Road, Flint. He married Sarah Ann Harrison on the 13th September 1902. They lived at 10 Swan Street, Flint. They had 2 children, John Edward and Mary Catherine. They later moved to 15 Evan Street, Flint.

Hugh had a big drink problem both in civilian life and in the army, for being drunk.

The County Herald reported: 3rd April 1903

Hugh James, 24 years of age, and residing at Commercial Road, was brought up on a charge of being drunk and disorderly on the 24th March. P.C. Davies proved the case and there was a long list of convictions against the defendant since 1895. The Mayor said the Bench had decided to fine him 5 shillings and costs or 14 days, and to place him on the black list, where he would have 3 years in which to become a teetotaller. It was, he said, disgraceful that a young man like him should have allowed these cases against him.

Hugh enlisted in Flint on the 22nd March 1915, originally into the 17th Battalion. He was posted to the 1st Battalion on the 19th October 1917.

Whilst in Italy his drinking problem caused him more grief. On the 17th March 1918 he was absent from roll call, he was in Genoa, contrary to standing orders, and was drunk on returning to camp. For this he forfeited 2 days pay and was awarded 14 days field punishment No1. This involved being tied to a fixed structure, such as a carriage wheel, for up to 1 hour per day.

He was admitted to the 38th Stationary Hospital in Genoa on the 18th May 1918, suffering from hypermetropia. He rejoined his battalion on the 26th May.

He died of acute dilation of the heart on the 12th June 1918. He is buried at Montecchio Precalcino Communal Cemetery Extension, Vicenza. Plot 4, row B, grave 7.

The circumstances of his death:

Hugh was seen by an Italian soldier, staggering drunkenly down the road to the convent at Praglia. He was being helped by another soldier. He tried to help but Hugh pushed them both away. As it was raining heavily he left them to it. He said one was wearing eye glasses.

Leorin d'Emilio, an 11 year old Italian boy, witnessed Hugh fall into the fast flowing river and he was immediately carried away by the current. The British Military Police were informed of the incident.

The surgeon who carried out the post mortem said that there was no evidence of drowning so he must have died before, or as he fell into the water. The cause of death was described as acute dilation of the heart and may have been caused by the shock of falling into the water.

William Harold Collier

Private 242690 5th South Lancashire Regiment
Date of death: 15/1/1918
Age: 24

William was born in Hurdsfield, Macclesfield in April 1893. He lived with his mother Caroline at 278 Hurdsfield Road. By 1911 they had moved to 223 i Road. He was now a card lacer at a silk mill. He enlisted in Macclesfield at the same time as Joseph Maher (see previous entry). He died on the same day as Joseph, 15th January 1918. He is buried next to him at Bois Guillaume Communal Cemetery Extension. C 5b.

The circumstances of his death:

He died of acute alcohol poisoning at No8 Stationary Hospital, Rouen.

Frederick William Pyman

Sergeant 14551 12th Gloucestershire Battalion
Date of death: 23/3/1916
Age: 36

Fredrick was born in Ipswich in 1880. He lived with his father Edgar Brice, and his mother Ada Sarah at 8 Orchard Street, Ipswich. He married Mary Ellen Fey in January 1900 and they lived at Ashley House, Ashley Hill, St Paul's, Bristol. They had 4 children, Frederick, Gladys, Queenie & Elsie. He was a boot shop manager. They later moved to 15 Manor Road, Bishopston, Bristol.

Frederick enlisted in Bristol. He died on the 23rd March 1916. He is buried at Habarcq Communal Cemetery Extension, Pas De Calais, France. I L6.

The circumstances of his death:

He was accidentally shot and killed by Armourer Private Cotterell, who was cleaning his rifle.

Alexander Grant

Driver T4/262095 Army Service Corps
Date of death: 17/9/1917

Alexander was born in Southport, Lancashire in 1898. He lived with his father James and mother Clara at 36 Railway Terrace, Southport. He was a motor mechanic. He enlisted in Southport. He died at Norfolk War Hospital, Norwich

The circumstances of his death:
The Southport Visiter reported:

Driver Grant died in the war hospital at Norwich, after having been admitted the previous day in an unconscious condition, following a kick on the head from a horse in the stables. He enlisted 12 months ago, and prior to that time was employed as a motor mechanic.

Robin Henderson

Private 2675 7th King's Liverpool Regiment
Date of death: 28/7/1915
Age: 20

Robin was born in Southport, Lancashire in 1895. He lived with his father Robert, a police sergeant, and his mother Nancy at 142 Norwood Road, Southport. They later moved to 23 Larch Street. He was an apprentice trimmer at Vulcan Motor Works. Robin enlisted in Southport on the 10th September 1914. He died on the 28th July 1915. He is buried at Duke Street Cemetery, Southport.

The circumstances of his death:

He drowned while bathing in the sea at Ramsgate along with Private Percy Henry Fletcher, also of the 2/7th Battalion, who went to rescue his comrade and also lost his life. Mr Robert Henderson, 23 Larch Street, Southport, an ex sergeant in the Borough Police Force, father of Private Henderson, received a letter from the commanding officer informing him of his son's death.

Private Henderson was a promising athlete and had won a silver cup only a week earlier at the Army & Navy Sports at Ramsgate, when he took first prize in the 100 yards race, and second prize in the quarter mile race.

John Livesley

Private 65219 14th Welsh Regiment
Died: 17/1/1919
Age: 20

John was born in Southport in 1898. He lived with his father James and mother Mary at 26a Oxford Road, Birkdale, Southport. He had a brother Richard. He was a gardener. He enlisted in Southport on the 15th February 1917. He suffered a gun shot wound to his left hand on the 19th September 1918. He also suffered from gas poisoning and a gun shot wound to his head. He died on the 17th January 1919. He is buried at Duke Street Cemetery, Southport.

The circumstances of his death:

He was knocked down by a train at Pool Hey crossing near Scarisbrick. He had been at Knowsley Park Hospital and was to be sent to Heaton Park to be demobilised. Prior to his death he was heard to mutter, " I might as well commit suicide as spend 19 years in the army.(He thought he was being sent to Russia with the army). There is nothing to live for now my mother and brother are dead." His brother had been killed in action the previous April. He walked along the line although knowing a train was due. His badly mutilated body was found on the line at Pool Hey crossing.

Herbert Leslie Monks

Private 302685 8th Manchester Regiment
Formerly 9092 Liverpool Regiment
Date of death: 6/7/1917
Age: 18

Herbert was born in Southport, Lancashire. He lived with his father Joseph Lawrence, and his mother Sarah Ann at 57 West Street, Southport. He enlisted in Southport, originally into the King's Liverpool Regiment. He died on the 6th July 1917. He is buried at Duke Street Cemetery, Southport.

The circumstances of his death:
The Southport Visiter reported:

Private Monks drowned while on bathing parade with other members of his battalion, near Scarborough. During the parade private Monks was missed, and his body was found the following day. The deceased was a good swimmer and it is thought he was overcome by a sand wave. He joined the Liverpool Scottish Regiment in September 1916 and transferred to the Manchester Regiment a few months later.

Prior to enlisting he was for some time an orderly at the Grange and Woodlands Hospital.

George Arundale

Private 55032   4th West Riding Regiment
Date of death: 26/5/1919

George was born in Middlesborough in 1900. He lived with his father George and mother Mary at 58 Egerton Street, Middlesborough. He had 3 brothers, Charles, Benjamin & William, and a sister Florence. He enlisted on the 26th June 1918.

George died on the 26th May 1919. He is buried at Cologne Southern Cemetery, Germany. IV A17

The circumstances of his death:

On the 26th May 1919, whilst on duty in Cologne, Germany, he was ordered to go to Ahrem with a horse drawn wagon. Whilst on the road a passing train startled the horses and he was thrown from the wagon. He was caught by the first carriage of the train, which dragged him along for about 3 metres. He was then caught by the 2nd carriage which ran him over, killing him instantly.

Alfred Mattison Wray

Sergeant 21447   20th Durham Light Infantry
Date of death: 6/4/1918

Alfred was born in Middlesborough. He lived with his mother Mary at 2 Hanson Street, Redcar. He had 4 brothers, Joseph, Arthur, James & Reginald, and 4 sisters, Alice, Emily, Ida & Edith. He was a clerk. He enlisted in Middlesborough on the 9th November 1914. He was appointed corporal on the 25th May 1915 and then to sergeant on the 22nd April 1916. He suffered a gun shot wound to his left shoulder on the 20th June 1917 and was treated at the 10th Casualty Clearing Station. He died on the 6th April 1918 at the 35th General Hospital.

The circumstances of his death:

Statement of Corporal Moody 239178   Royal Engineers

On Friday April 5th, at about 2.30pm an officer on a passing train shouted out that a man had fallen off and I and sappers Nock & Woolridge, ran back to find him. I did not reach the man until several minutes after the others. When I reached the place they had carried him clear of the rails and he was on one side of the track, dead. I went back towards camp to get a stretcher and eventually obtained one from the Anti Aircraft Camp at Northkerque. The body was carried back to Northkerque station and eventually to the Anti Aircraft Camp, as a medical officer stated that an ambulance could not be obtained that night.

Statement of Sapper Woolridge:

On Corporal Moody's instructions I ran back and found the body of a Durham Light Infantry sergeant lying across the left hand rail of the line with his feet and legs between the rails. His right arm and body were badly cut and he was obviously dead. I lifted the body on one side and helped carry him to the station. I then went back to my work.

Statement of Sergeant McCorry

I, along with the deceased, left Etaples on the morning of the 5th April 1918 to proceed to join the Battalion. We travelled in the train as far as Calais where same halted. At this halt he left the train to go to the latrine. Whilst away the train moved off after which I saw nothing of him.

He is buried at Les Baraques Military Cemetery, Sangatte, Pas De Calais, France. III D3.

David Anderson Alexander

Driver T4/043141 501st Horse Transport Company
Army Service Corps
Date of death: 22/4/1919

David was born in Burntisland, Fife in 1885. He lived with his father David and mother Elizabeth. He had 5 brothers, Benjamin, John, Stewart, William & George, and 4 sisters, Barbara, Annie, Catherine & Elizabeth. He married Janet on the 14th September 1908 and they lived at 16 Shore Street. They had 5 children, John, Minnie, Violet, Minnie & David.

David enlisted in Greenock on the 17th January 1915. He entered France on the 29th August 1915. He died on the 22nd April 1919. He is buried at Les Baraques Military Cemetery, Sangatte, Pas De Calais, France. XVIII A 8A.

The circumstances of his death:

He was knocked down and killed by a train on the main Nord line Boulogne to Calais, near Dinant.

Thomas Middleton Hulme

Staff Sergeant 184987 Royal Engineers
Formerly 20134 King's Liverpool Regiment
Date of death: 26/5/1919
Age: 35

Thomas lived with his wife Jane at 6 Deepfield Road, Wavertree, Liverpool. He enlisted in Liverpool, originally into the King's Liverpool Regiment. He was later transferred to the Royal Engineers. He died on the 26th May 1919. He is buried at Blargues Communal Cemetery |Extension, Oise, France. III E6.

The circumstances of his death:

He died from a fractured skull after trying, and failing to beat a train across a level crossing.

David Clarke

Lance corporal 9714 2nd Black Watch
Date of death: 11/7/1915

David was born in Dunfermline, Fifeshire, Scotland. He was married to Helen. He enlisted in Dunfermline. He died on the 11th July 1915. He is buried at St Vaast Post Military Cemetery, Pas De Calais, France. I D10.

The circumstances of his death:

He impaled himself on his own bayonet whilst getting into the trench under heavy fire.

William Claude Burdekin

Private 786 Lancashire Hussars Yeomanry
Date of death: 23/12/1914

William was born in St Helens, Lancashire in 1893. He lived with his father William, a mechanical engineer, and his mother Charlotte at 139 Boundary Road, St Helens. He was a joiner at Pilkington Brothers. He enlisted in St Helens on the 28th February 1913. He died on the 23rd December 1914. He is buried at St Helens Cemetery.

The circumstances of his death:

Whilst eating his dinner he swallowed his false teeth and was taken to hospital. He was admitted to the 1st Western General Hospital. There was a court of enquiry into the cause of his death as there was a report of a biscuit being forced into his mouth which caused him to swallow his teeth.

Richard White

Private 9069 1st Royal Welsh Fusiliers
Date of death: 19/6/1917
Age: 37

Richard was born in Birmingham in 1888. He lived with his father Richard, a coal carter, and his mother Sophia at 8 Powell Street, Aston Manor, Birmingham. He had a brother William and a sister Elizabeth. He was a newsagent. He enlisted in Birmingham on the 15th March 1906. He served in Burma and India. He entered France on the 11th August 1914. He suffered gun shot wounds to his head and chest on the 4th May 1917. He was admitted to No 23 Field Ambulance and then on to No49 Casualty Clearing Station, and finally to No6 General Hospital at Rouen. He rejoined his battalion on the 4th June 1917. He died on the 19th June 1917. He is buried at Achiet-Le-Grand Communal Cemetery Extension, Pas De Calais, France.

The circumstances of his death:

There was a court of enquiry into his death. Captain G.E. Chappell, Royal Army Medical Corps states:
"At about 7am on the 19th inst. I was called to a tent in the transport lines. I found No6849 Private Ashdown, No8491 Private T Pickering (see following entries) and No 9069 Private R White lying on the ground, motionless.
I examined them and found them to be dead.
No6849 private Ashdown had his head and face burnt, No9069 Private White had his arm burnt. No8491 Private T Pickering was burn about the head and body. The 5 wounded men were found to be suffering from burns & shock. I consider that the above deaths & injuries were due to lightning during a thunderstorm."

Edward Ashdown
Private 6849   1st Royal Welsh Fusiliers
Date of death: 19/6/1917

Edward was born in Birmingham in 1883. He lived with his father Henry & mother Mary at 4 Hamilton Buildings, Monument Road. He had 2 brothers, Edwin & Thomas, and 6 sisters, Annie, Sarah, Marie, Nelly, May & Maud. He later married Annie.

He enlisted in Birmingham in 1914. He entered France on the 21st September 1914. He was killed by lightning on the 19th June 1917. He is buried alongside Richard White (see previous entry) at Achiet Le Grand Communal Cemetery Extension, Pas De Calais, France. I L30.

Thomas Pickering
Private 8491 1st Royal Welsh Fusiliers
Date of death: 19/6/1917

Thomas was born in Bradwell Grove, Oxon. He lived with his father William. He was killed by lightning on the 19th June 1917. He is buried alongside Edward Ashdown (see previous entry|) at Achiet Le Grand Communal Cemetery Extension, Pas De Calais, France. I L29.

Daniel Coombes

Corporal 8161 3rd Duke Of Cornwall's Light Infantry
Date of death: 30/5/16
Age: 28

Daniel was born in St Giles, London in 1888. He had a brother Michael & a sister Margaret. He enlisted in Holborn, London. He entered France on the 29th August 1914. He died on the 30th May 1916. He is buried at St Saviour Roman Catholic Churchyard, Totland, Isle Of Wight.

The circumstances of his death:

He was struck by lightning during a heavy thunderstorm on the Isle Of Wight.

Edward Perry Townsend
Lance corporal 29145 Royal Army Medical Corps
Date of death: 7/6/1916

Percy was born in London. He was killed by lightning whilst sitting under an oak tree during a thunderstorm at Cookham.

Stanley Galloway Allen
Driver   Army Service Corps
Date of death: 7/7/1915

The Times 8/7/1915:

Stanley Galloway Allen, aged 36, of Hull, Yorkshire, a driver with the Army Service Corps, was struck by lightning during a thunderstorm yesterday. The lightning struck his cap and he was killed instantly.

Francis Elliott
Rifleman 10709 6th Royal Irish Rifles
Date of death: 18/6/1917
Age: 32

Francis was born in Belfast in 1885. He lived with his father George and mother Jane at 21 Oregon Street, Belfast. He enlisted in Belfast.
He was killed by lightning on the 18th June 1917. He is buried at Lahana Military Cemetery, Thessalonika.

Alexander McKeachie

Private 1220 5th King's Own Scottish Borderers
Date of death: 4/8/1915.

Alexander was born in Whithorn, Wigtownshire, Scotland. He lived with his father Andrew and mother Margaret at 81 George Street, Whithorn. He enlisted in Whithorn, into the 5th Battalion King's Own Scottish Borderers. He died on the 4th August 1915. He is buried at Alexandria Cemetery. K54.

The circumstances of his death:

The Wigtownshire Free Press 2 /9/15

Alexander McKeachie, serving with the King's Own Scottish Borderers Transport Division in the Dardanelles, was tragically drowned whilst off duty. His parents, who live in St John Street, received the terrible news initially from the War Office, and later more details were revealed in a letter from his sergeant, John Cain, who writes,

"Just a note to let you know the details of poor Alexander's death. After our stables duties and early morning exercise, we were clear from 8.30am to noon. In that free time nearly every man goes bathing.

It is so hot we are glad to get into the water. Another man seemed to be in difficulties. Alexander bravely went to his assistance and was in the act of reaching him when a big wave swept right past. Alexander was then in difficulties himself. Two other men managed to reach them both and pulled them to shore. Johnstone quickly recovered but Alexander did not.

He was taken to hospital but the next day we received news that he had died without ever regaining consciousness.

Ernest Ball

Private 331274 18th Royal Warwickshire Regiment
Date of death: 2/7/1917
Age: 18

Ernest was born in Coventry, Warwickshire in 1899. He lived with his father Thomas and mother Milly at 20 Albert Street, Coventry. They later moved to 31 Spencer Street. He enlisted in Coventry on the 31st March 1917. He died on the 2nd July 1917. He is buried at Ipswich Old Cemetery, Suffolk. D28 34.

The circumstances of his death:

Soldier's Fatal Swerve

At the Ranelagh Road Hospital, Ipswich, on Tuesday, the Borough Coroner investigated the tragic death of a young private, named Ernest Bell, who was killed at bayonet practice on July 2nd.

The accident was described by Sergeant John Plimmer. On Monday afternoon the sergeant was instructing a class, which included the deceased, in a simple form of bayonet practice. The men had to leave one trench, make a point at some sacks ten paces further on, and then drop into another trench. They had done this once, and after pointing out one or two minor faults, witness told them to do it again, warning them to remain in line and to keep correct distances from each other. Witness stood at the sacks and saw that each man passed to the left of the sacks correctly.

After that he saw the men go into the trench ten yards further on. They were not quite in line and the deceased seemed rather late. Just as he descended the sergeant heard someone shout "Oh!".

He ran down the trench immediately, and as he jumped into it Private Phipps shouted, "He has jumped on my bayonet." He found the deceased lying with a wound in the right side of his throat and bleeding profusely from the mouth.

He got him out of the trench and sent for medical aid, which arrived almost immediately. Witness had taken every precaution to avert an accident, and if the deceased had alighted in his proper place the fatality would not have happened. Witness had had considerable experience in bayonet training and had no previous fatal accidents of this kind. Prior to the accident he had complimented the deceased on his good work- he was a very smart little chap. He passed the sacks at the proper distance and must have deviated to the right at the last moment. He was, no doubt, on top of the bayonet before the man using it could place it in the proper position. He believed Phipps got into his proper position.

Private Ernest Charles Phipps corroborated the sergeant's story and said the first thing he knew after jumping into the trench was that the deceased was on his bayonet. The bayonet went 3 or 4 inches into the deceased's neck and he bled very copiously.

Samuel Hosselby Garrett

Private 3065 5th Royal Warwickshire Regiment
Date of death: 15/7/1915
Age: 17

Samuel was born in Coventry in 1899. He lived with his father George and mother Eliza at 18 Broomfield Road, Coventry. He had 3 brothers, John, Thomas & Charles, and 2 sisters, Alice & Maggie. He enlisted in Coventry. He died on the 15th July 1915. He is buried at London Road Cemetery, Coventry.

The circumstances of his death:

He drowned whilst bathing at Chelmsford.

Charles Goodyear

Driver T4/ 071627 Army Service Corps
Horse Transport Depot
Date of death: 18/6/1915

Charles was born in Andover, Hampshire. He lived at 6 Park Cottages, Andover. He drowned whilst on service in Egypt. He is buried at Alexandria Military Cemetery, Egypt. L114.

Albert Rigby

Private 30058 8th Royal Welsh Fusiliers
Date of death: 1/5/1916
Age: 28

Albert was born in Liverpool on the 5th December 1887. He lived with his father Thomas, a shipwright, and his mother Eleanor at 24 Fletcher Street, Toxteth Park, Liverpool. He married Mary Roberts on the 22nd November 1909 and they lived at 68 South Ashton Street, Liverpool. They had 2 sons, Robert & Albert. He enlisted in Liverpool on the 25th June 1915. He died on the 1st May 1916. He is buried at Amara War Cemetery, Iraq. XX A6.

The circumstances of his death:

He was cleaning his rifle and placed the muzzle on his knee without realising it was still loaded. Whilst using a cleaning brush on the bolt action he pulled the safety catch forward and shot himself in the knee, the bullet passing through his knee and into his foot. He died at a field hospital the following day.

John Ware

Segeant 2328 5th Notts & Derby Regiment
The Sherwood Foresters
Date of death: 7/3/1915

John was born in Hanley, Staffordshire in 1884. He lived with his father William & mother Elizabeth. He married Eliza Ann Lawton on the 25th December 1903. They lived at 23 Bernard Street, Burton-On-Trent. He was a sanitary pipe labourer. They had 2 sons, William & John. He enlisted in Derby on the 8th August 1914. He died on the 7th March 1915 ant No10 Field Ambulance. He is buried at London Rifle Brigade Cemetery, Comines-Warneton, Belgium.

The circumstances of his death:

He was under trench instruction when he was hit by a bullet from an accidental discharge from one of his own men. He died the same day.

Fred Frazer

Private 59030 West Yorkshire Regiment
Date of death: 14/1/1918

Fred was born in Oxenhope, Yorkshire on the 24th December 1898. He lived with his father Bert & mother Ada at 7 Ash Street, Oxenhope. He was a painter & decorator. He enlisted in Keighley, Yorkshire on the 24th April 1917. He died on the 14th January 1918. He buried at Oxenhope Cemetery. II 411.

The circumstances of his death:

He and another soldier were practising rapid loading with dummy cartridges. A live cartridge had got mixed in amongst them. Fred was struck in the head and died immediately.

Harold Ackerley

Private 291564 10th Welsh Regiment
Date of death: 24/12/1917

Harold was born in Salford, Lancashire. He lived with his father Alfred Vernon and his mother Clementina at 17 Regent Square, Salford. He enlisted in Manchester. He died on the 24th December 1917. He is buried at Rue David Military Cemetery, Flerbaix, Pas De Calais, France.

The circumstances of his death:

He was accidentally shot after cleaning his rifle. He was handling the rifle butt end first, and had forgotten to apply the safety catch. He shot himself in both legs. He died shortly afterwards at a field hospital.

Walter Everall Ennion

Sergeant M2/028566 Army Service Corps
Date of death: 27/5/1917

Walter was born in Salford, Lancashire in 1891. He lived with his father Thomas Frederick and mother Clara at Regent Hotel, Regent Road, Salford. He had 5 brothers, Thomas, Frederick, Henry, Charles & Lawrence, and 2 sisters, Gertrude & Annie. He enlisted in Salford on the 16th February 1915. He died on the 27th May 1917. He is buried at Mikra British Cemetery, Greece.

The circumstances of his death:

He was burnt to death when a candle was knocked over in a tent in which he was sleeping.

Fergus Milton Kay

Private M2/031641 Army Service Corps
Date of death: 5/5/1915

Fergus was born Shuttleworth, Lancashire in 1893. He lived with his father John Thomas, and mother Bessie at 5 Irwell Terrace, Bacup, Lancashire. He had 3 brothers, Henry, Richard & Frederick, and 2 sisters, Gertrude & Martha. By 1911 he was living at 98 Manchester Road, Bury. He was a motor lorry driver. He enlisted in London on the 23rd December 1914. He died on the 5th May 1915. He is buried at Desvres Communal Cemetery, Pas De Calais, France.

The circumstances of his death:

He died in a motorcycle accident. A court of enquiry was held:

1st witness: No Sr/860 Driver Turner, T, ASC Reserve Park states, "About 7.50pm on the 5th May I met Pte Kay on his motorcycle, just as he was going to start from Desvres. He asked me if I would like to go for a ride with him and I said yes. We reached Senlecques all right and Pte Kay handed over his despatches to a despatch rider there. We started on our return journey at about 8pm and everything went well until we reached the fork in the road at the foot of the hill leading into Desvres. It was fairly light at the time and as we turned the bend of the road at the foot of the hill I remember seeing a cart with a white horse approaching us about 150 yards ahead.
 Private Kay sounded the horn all the way down the hill, and was riding on his right side of the road.
 I don't remember anything more till I woke up and found myself lying on a low bank on the left side of the road, and the cycle lying beside me.
 On getting up I looked round and saw Private Kay lying about 15 yards behind me on the bank on the left hand side of the road.

I tried to lift him up but could not. He just gave one groan and lay still. I did not see any sign of the cart and white horse after the accident. Immediately afterwards the Medical Officer came up. He asked me if I was hurt and I said I was all right. I also told him I had been out riding with Private Kay. He then told me to go back to my billet. At the time the accident happened Private Kay was going at a very fast rate. It was the second time I had been out riding with him."

2nd Evidence: Monsieur Tintillier (through an interpreter) states: " I was returning home from Desvres at about 8pm. My home is on the road between Desvres and Senleqcues. When I was about 150 yards from the bend in the road where it forks at the foot of the hill, a motor bicycle came round the corner, going very fast. He was going so fast he could not get over to his right side of the road before he met my cart, so he swerved to the left and tried to pass between my cart and the fence. He ran against my right shaft and was thrown backwards into the middle of the road. I tied my horse to a tree and picked him up carried him to the side of the road. As I saw the man was badly hurt I immediately returned to Desvres to get a doctor. It was fairly light at the time and I heard no horn sounded. I saw a second man lying on the road but he got up after a few minutes and seemed all right."

Denis Whalem

Canadian Expeditionary Force
Date of death: 1917

Circumstances of his death:

Newspaper report:
Private James Bennett, CEF, stated that on Thursday night at about 8.30 he went to the rifle range at trhe Fun City, Gracehill, Kent, England. The range was one where anyone could shoot and was in the charge of a lady. At this time there were 3 men firing, including himself. Witnesses saw Joyce pick up his rifle and fire one shot at the target.

He then unloaded his rifle and began to reload. At this point the deceased spoke to him, and Joyce at once turned bodily to him, and the rifle went off. The rifle was then pointing towards the deceased, who fell up against a wall as soon as the discharge took place. One of the girls held him up and they undid his tunic, finding he had been shot in the chest. The manager was fetched and on seeing what had happened, provided a taxi.

Witness though the deceased was speaking quietly to Joyce whilst he was unloading, causing him to turn round, rifle and all.

Clarence McCabe

Private 835648 4th Canadian Mounted Rifles
Date of death: 26/5/1917

Clarence was born in Napanee, Ontario On the 23rd June 1891. He lived with his father Ashton and mother Martha. He enlisted on the 1st March 1916 into the 146th Battalion. He arrived in England on the 8th October 1916. He was transferred to the 4th Canadian Mounted Rifles on the 30th November. On the day of his death they were in reserve at Toronto Camp. He died on the 26th May 1917.

The circumstances of his death:

At about 8.30pm on May 26th 1917, while playing a game of baseball when his Battalion was in Divisional Reserve, near Vimy Ridge, he picked up a shell, which exploded (cause unknown). He was killed along with 7 others (see following entries). He is buried at La Targette British Cemetery, Neuville St Vaast, Pas De Calais, France.

Arthur Carroll

Private 835475 4th Canadian Mounted Rifles
Date of death: 27/5/1917

Arthur was born in Conway, Ontario on the 7th February 1895. He enlisted in Kingston, Ontario on the 25th January 1915. He died on the 27th May 1917 after being involved in an explosion during a baseball game (see previous entry). He is buried at Barlin Communal Cemetery Extension.

Bert James Travis

Private 838702 4th Canadian Mounted Rifles
Date of death: 26/5/1917

Bert was born in Wareham, Dorset on the 5th January 1897. He later emigrated to Ontario, Canada. He enlisted on the 22nd January 1916. He was killed on the 26th May 1917 along with 6 others, in an explosion during a baseball game near Vimy Ridge.

George Fraser Griffin
Private 648376 4th Canadian Mounted Rifles
Date of death: 26/5/1917

George was born in West Stockbridge, Massachusetts, USA on the 30th June 1897. He emigrated to Canada with his parents, George and Ethel in 1900. He enlisted on the 26th January 1916. He was killed by an explosion during a baseball game.

Charles Hartin
Private 636730 4th Canadian Mounted Rifles
Date of death: 26/5/1917

Charles was born in Marlbank, Ontario on the 12th February 1898. He lived with his father Christopher and mother Agnes. He enlisted on the 16th January 1916. He died in an explosion during a baseball match.

Edwin Payne
Private 727325 4th Canadian Mounted Rifles
Date of death: 26/5/1917

Edwin was born in Surrey on the 23rd May 1895. He lived with his father Thomas and his mother Alice. He enlisted in Stratford, Ontario on the 29th December 1915. He was killed on the 26th May 1917 after an explosion during a baseball match.

James Henry Dunn

Private 835508 4th Canadian Mounted Rifles
Date of death: 26/5/1917

James was born in Napanee, Ontario on the 19th May 1894. He lived with his father William and mother Isabelle. He enlisted in Kingston, Ontario on the 19th January 1916. He was killed by an explosion during a baseball match.

Shurley Asselstine

Private   4th Canadian Mounted Rifles
Date of death: 26/5/1917

Shurley was born in Napanee, Ontario on the 3rd May 1893. He enlisted on the 19th February 1916. He was killed by an explosion during a baseball match.

George Abbey

Private 9879 3rd Battalion Canadian Infantry
Date of death: 14/6/1916
Age: 45

  He was accidentally shot by No9901 Private J Denoon. He and Private Abbey were cooks in D Company Wagon. Denoon was handling a rifle which had come down from the trenches when it went off, the bullet going through Abbey's neck. He died almost instantly. It appears that there was a cartride in the barrel of the rifle, and that the lock was so caked in mud that it would not open, which was the reason the owner never unloaded it.

  He is buried at Brandhoek Military Cemetery, Poperinghe, Belgium.

Joseph Orrick

Private 1738 Princess Patricia's Canadian Light Infantry
Date of death: 12/8/1916
Age: 32

Joseph was born in Durham. He lived with his wife Elizabeth Ann at 907, 10th Street, Calgary, Alberta. They later moved to 1346 Harrison Street, Victoria, British Columbia. He enlisted on the 28th August 1914. He died on the 12th August 1916. He is buried at Youngstown Cemetery, Alberta.

The circumstances of his death:

He accidentally shot himself while trying to club a rabbit with the butt of his rifle.

Loring Brooks Adams

Lieutenant Canadian Engineers
Date of death: 22/6/1918

Loring was born in Ontario on the 15th July 1888. He lived with his father John & mother Amy at Wales, Ontario. He was a civil engineer. He enlisted on the 19th April 1916. He died on the 22nd June 1918. He is buried at Huby St Ieu British Cemetery, Pas De Calais, France.

The circumstances of his death:

Whilst crossing a level crossing at Aubin St Vaast at or before 2.40am on the 22nd June 1918, he was struck by a west bound train, receiving injuries- lacerated right arm (amputated) lacerated skull, abrasions to body & legs from which he died at 8.45am at No59 Casualty Clearing Station, the same day.

George Vallance Aitken

Gunner 85650 12th Brigade Canadian Field Artillery
Date of death: 12/10/1916

George was born in Edinburgh, Scotland on the 28th July 1895. He later emigrated to Canada. He enlisted on the 8th February 1915. He died on the 12th October 1916. He is buried at Dartmoor Cemetery, Becordel, France.

The circumstances of his death:

On October 12th 1916 this soldier was granted permission to visit his brother in the RCHA. The following morning he was absent and several inquiries were made in that vicinity, but we could find no trace of him. On October 17th information was received from No37 Field Ambulance, stating that this soldier had been admitted there on 12th October suffering from injuries received by being run over by a motor lorry, and that he had died there the same night. It is presumed that he was getting a lift on a motor lorry and was in some way run over.

James Aitken

Private 769314 18th Battalion Canadian Infantry
Date of death: 23/12/1916
Age: 19

James was born in Edinburgh on the 15th August 1897. He lived with his mother Jemima at 82 Kenneth Avenue, Toronto. He was a clerk at Messrs Eaton & Co, Toronto. He enlisted in Toronto on the 29th December 1915. He died on the 23rd December 1916. He is buried at Bois De Noulette British Cemetery, France.

The circumstances of his death:

This soldier was one of a working party attached to the 6th Field Company Canadian Engineers, for duty at Aix Noulette. This place was shelled and the concussion injured one of the walls of the cookhouse which the party were using , and while the men were lined up getting a meal, the wall suddenly collapsed, killing Private Aitken and one other man.

Morton Bostwick Allen

Private 60111   21st Battalion Canadian Infantry
Date of death: 2/12/1916
Age: 38

Morton was born in Kingston, Ontario on the 3rd September 1878. He enlisted at Sandling Camp in England on the 19th July 1915. His wife Minne was living at 425 Fell Street, San Francisco, USA. He died on the 2nd December 1916 at No2 Canadian Casualty Clearing Station. He is buried at Ljissenthoek Military Cemetery, Poperinghe, Belgium.

The circumstances of his death:

He was accidentally run over by an ambulance on the main road between Lille Gate & Zillebeke, on the night of 2nd December 1916, receiving injuries (contused scalp & 5 fractured ribs) from which he died.

Frank Lidington Aldous MM

Lance Sergeant 706137   54th Battalion British Columbia Regiment
Date of death: 15/4/1919

Frank was born in Brackley, Northamptonshire on the 4th November 1891. He lived with his father Robert & mother Selina at 8 Ellesmere Terrace, Brackley. He later emigrated to Canada. He enlisted on the 8th December 1915. He was awarded the Military Medal. He died on the 15th April 1919. He is buried at Hoeylaert Communal Cemetery, Belgium.

The circumstances of his death:

He suffered a self inflicted gun shot wound to his right temple.

William Sharpe Baillie

Lieutenant 87th Battalion
Date of death: 13/5/1918

William was struck by an engine on the light railway near Mingohal, receiving injuries from which he subsequently died at No 57 Casualty Clearing Station on the 13th May 1918. He suffered pneumonia as a result of exposure after his accident. He is buried at Aubigny Communal Cemetery Extension.

Stephen Baldwin

Private 115855   Canadian Light Horse
Date of death: 8/2/1918
Age: 35

Stephen was born in London, England on the 6th October 1882. He was accidentally killed on the 8th February 1918 by a bullet fired from the rifle of Private 860 R.A. Whitfield. He is buried at Aux Riets Military Cemetery.

William John Ball

Gunner 42437 3rd Brigade Canadian Field Artillery
Date of death: 13/2/1915

William was born in Farringdon, Berkshire on the 22nd July 1869. He later emigrated to Canada. He lived with his wife Annie at 128 Seneca Street, Fairbank, York, Ontario. He enlisted in Valcartier, Quebec on the 22nd September 1914. He died on the 13th February 1915. He suffered a fractured skull while on board HMT Australind.

George Simpson Bannister

Acting Sergeant 12828   1st Divisional HQ
Date of death: 30/10/1915
Age: 41

George was born in Blackburn, Lancashire on the 2nd January 1874. Before enlisting he was a clerk with the 16th Light Horse. He enlisted enlisted in Valcartier, Quebec on the 18th September 1914. He died on the 30th October 1915. He is buried at Rosenberg Chateau Military Cemetery, Ploegsteert.

The circumstances of his death:

He met his death as a result of shooting himself with his rifle during temporary insanity brought on by worry over personal affairs.

John Bannister

Private 877187 25th Battalion Canadian Expeditionary Force
Date of death: 30/3/1918
Age: 26

John was born on the 6th December 1891. he died on the 30th March 1918. He is buried at Doullen Communal Cemetery.

The circumstances of his death:

Whilst in the trenches he was accidentally shot. He died of his wounds at No3 Canadian Stationary Hospital.

Marcus George Bardwell

Private 2755 Canadian Army Service Corps
2nd Divisional Supply Column
Date of death: 6/11/1915

Marcus was born in London, England on the 28th February 1882. He was a chauffuer. He enlisted in Toronto on the 2nd February 1915. He died on the 6th November 1915. He is buried at Bailleul Communal Cemetery Extension, France.

The circumstances of his death:

He died at No2 Casualty Clearing Station as a result of fractured ribs & clavicle sustained through a railway accident.

Joseph Barnes

Private 684751 38th Company Canadian Forestry Corps
Date of death: 25/6/1918

He was killed by a falling tree. He is buried at St Leonard's Cemetery, Alencon, France.

James Rueben Scott

Regimental Sergeant Major 35304 Canadian Army Service Corps 1st Reserve Park
Date of death: 19/8/1916
Age: 43

James was born in London, England on the 30th December 1872. He later emigrated to Canada. He lived with his wife Alice at 7460 St Dominique Street, Montreal. He enlisted in Valcartier, Quebec on the 22nd September 1914. He died on the 19th August 1916.

The circumstances of his death:

At 7pm on the 19th August 1916, he was in the act of mounting the picquet and had called out "fall in the picquet and the guard", when he was willfully shot by a soldier of his own unit. The medical officer was on the spot within a minute but could do nothing to save his life, the bullet having gone through his chest. He died in a few minutes.

The soldier who shot him was Driver Benjamin Defehr 2062 Army Service Corps. He was later tried for murder and was executed on the 25th August 1916.

Thomas Henry Fagan
Private 2393387   Canadian Machine Gun Corps
Date of death: 7/6/1918
Age: 19

Thomas was born in Manchester, England on the 12th February 1899. He later emigrated to the USA. He lived with his father Alfred, and mother Mary at 1039 Avenue D, College Point, Queen's County, New York. He died on the 7th June 1918. He is buried at Huby St Leu British Cemetery, France.

The circumstances of his death:

He was accidentally killed during a course of machine gun instruction at Guisy Camp. There was live ammunition mixed in with the dummy ammunition.

Lawrence Caffrey

Lieutenant 8th Brigade Canadian Field Artillery
Date of death: 7/3/1918

Circumstances of his death:

At about 2am on the 7th March 1918 his servants woke up and found that the officer's shack was on fire. They made a hole in the side of the shack but flames came out and they could hear nothing. It was soon a mass of flames and nothing could be done to put it out. The bodies of Lt Caffrey and another officer were found near the door which they were evidently unable to open before being overcome by the smoke. The cause of the fire is unknown. He is buried at Ecoivres Military Cemetery, Pas De Calais, France.

William McClure Calder

Captain Canadian Forestry Company
Date of death: 1/11/1918

William was born in Lachute, Quebec, Canada on the 6th October 1896. His father was George. He joined Princess Patricia's Canadian Light Infantry on the 8th July 1915. He was invalided out due to either wounds or sickness. He re-enlisted on the 19th September 1916. He died on the 1st November 1918.

The circumstances of his death:

He was killed when the motorcycle he was riding collided with a motor lorry coming in the opposite direction.

Augustus Frank Cameron

Acting Staff Sergeant Canadian Army Service Corps
Date of death: 12/8/1917

Circumstances of his death:

While on a motorcycle, in the pursuance of military duties, he collided with a horse in the town on Lugos, Gironde, at 8.15pm on the 12th August 1917. The cycle came in contact with the horse, which was unattended on the road, and he was thrown from the cycle and was instantly killed.

He is buried Talence Communal Cemetery Extension, Bordeaux, France.

Alfred McDonald Campbell

Private 743 Canadian Army Service Corps
4th Divisional Supply Column
Date of death: 21/12/1916

Circumstances of his death:

He died of rupture and internal haemorrhage caused through being run over by a truck. He was dead on arrival at No6 Canadian Field Ambulance.

A court of enquiry found that Private Campbell was accidentally killed while in performance of his duties and while safe guarding traffic, and the contributory cause was a defective headlight and that no blame could be attached to the driver of the truck.

He is buried at Barlin Communal Cemetery Extension, Pas De Calais, France.

David Emmett Coyne

Sergeant 3347   31st Battalion Australian Imperial Force
Date of death: 15/8/1918

David was born in Marian, Queensland, Australia. He enlisted in Rockhampton, Queensland on the 25th January 1916. He embarked at Hobart, Tasmania on the 10th May 1916 and disembarked at Suez on the 15th June. He was promoted to sergeant on the 17th December 1916. He qualified as a bombing instructor on the 16th June 1917. He died on the 15th August 1918 at the 61st Casualty Clearing Station. He is buried at Vignacourt Military Cemetery, France.

The circumstances of his death:

As he was throwing a bomb from the trench he either slipped or caught his hand on the parapet. The bomb dropped into the bottom of the trench. He shouted "Get out of the trench, there's a live bomb in it". He threw himself on top of the bomb as it exploded. He died of wounds received in that explosion at the 61st Casualty Clearing Station on the 15th August 1918.

David Coyne's original grave marker.

He was posthumously awarded the Albert Medal on the 22nd October 1918 for his actions in saving his fellow comrades.

Percy Norman

Private 1335 1st Australian Cyclists Corps
Date of death: 17/10/1918

Percy was born in Colac, Victoria in 1893. He enlisted in Melbourne, Victoria on the 21st July 1915. He died on the 17th October 1918. He is buried at St Pierre Cemetery, Amiens, France.

The circumstances of his death:

On the 17th October Private Norman & Private Cook, who were on attachment from Unit, acting as guards in the Corps Vegetable Garden, rode on their cycles to Amiens. They were returning along the canal towpath and were the worse for drink. Private Norman swerved and rode into the canal and was drowned. Private Cook tried to rescue him but was unable to do so.

Arthur Poyntz Hirst

Trooper 1539 3rd Light Horse
Date of death: 22/6/1916

Arthur was born in Hobart, Tasmania in 1896. He enlisted in Claremont, Tasmania on the 19th August 1915. He died on the 22nd June 1916. He is buried at Calais Cemetery, British Section.

The circumstances of his death:

He was found on a level crossing near Calais on the 21st June 1916 and was taken to the 35th General Hospital, Calais, where he died the next day of a fractured skull.

Statement made by Gunner P Carlyson:

On June 21st 1916 I was to proceed from Havre to Caestre by train, in charge of 8 mules, with 1 other man. I did not feel well and at one station the train stopped I got out and asked Sergeant Major Smith for extra help. I think that was between 9 and 10pm. He detailed one man to assist me, and as the train moved out of the station Trooper Hirst missed his own and got into my truck. About 10 minutes later, owing to the swaying of the truck, the 4 mules at the end fell, and Trooper Hurst was standing by the door, which had jammed and was half open, the left hand mule, in getting up, struck him on the body with one of his fore feet, and knocked him backwards out of the door. I immediately looked out and saw him lying clear of the line in a heap. The train was travelling at about 40 miles per hour. There was no means of communicating with the driver or guard. At the next stop I reported the occurrence at the first opportunity.

Harold Clifford Brooke

Private 1826 3rd Pioneer Battalion
Date of death: 19/1/1917

Harold was born in Melbourne, Victoria in 1896. He lived with his father George at "Athelstane", Dalesbury Avenue, Ivanhoe, Victoria. He was an electrical mechanic. He enlisted in Melbourne on the 25th May 1916. He embarked at Melbourne on the 23rd July 1916 and disembarked at Plymouth, England on the 11th September 1916. He died on the 19th January 1917. He is buried at Cite Bonjean Military Cemetery, Armentieres, France.

The circumstances of his death:

He was in charge of the maintenance of a power station and was accidentally electrocuted whilst cleaning a switch board.

Alfred William Askew

Sergeant 11199 3rd Divisional Ambulance Workshop
Date of death: 25/12/1918

Alfred was born in Ballarat, Victoria in 1890. He lived with his father Michael at 38 Weller Street, Geelong, West Victoria. He was a motor engineer. He enlisted in Melbourne on the 25th February 1916. He died on the 25th December 1918.

He is buried at Civilian Cemetery, Morville, Belgium.

The circumstances of his death:

He was electrocuted whilst doing wiring work in the workshops. He fell a distance of 8 feet from his ladder, sustaining severe head injuries, including a fractured skull. Both hands and forearms were badly burned. He died at 13th Field Ambulance.

William Orr

Private 3178 25th Battalion Australian Imperial Force
Date of death: 30/12/1915

William was born in Paisley, Scotland in 1889. He enlisted in Roma, Queensland on the 17th August 1915. He died on the 30th December 1915.

The circumstances of his death:

William fell from the rigging on board the troop ship "Itonis".

Statement from William Kelly, senior medical officer on board HMAT "Itonis":

"At about 2.50pm on the 30th December 1915, I was summoned to attend an accident to No 3178 Pte W Orr, of the 25th Battalion Australian Imperial Force. I found life to be extinct. There was a large scalp wound of recent origin on the back of Orr's head, and blood was coming his mouth and nose. He evidently had a fractured skull. A fall of 8 or 10 feet could have caused the injury. As far as I can tell there was no suspicious circumstances connected with the event."

Joseph Vincent Cicalese

Private 2253 29th Battalion Australian Imperial Force
Date of death: 29/12/1917

Joseph was born in Melbourne, Victoria. He lived with his mother Phoebe at 287 Barkley Street, St Kilda, Victoria. He enlisted in Balaclave, Victoria on the 24th September 1917. He died on the 29th December 1917.

The circumstances of his death:

The end of an awning spar on the troopship he was on fell on top of him, causing a fractured skull.

Reginald Arthur Beard

Gunner 2384 3rd Brigade Field Artillery
Date of death: 9/7/1916

Reginald was born in Cheltenham, England. He enlisted at Brisbane, Queensland on the 1st September 1914. He embarked at Brisbane on the 25th September 1914. He died on the 9th July 1916.

The circumstances of his death:

Whilst off duty in Egypt he went to climb a pyramid and fell about 15 feet and was rendered unconscious. He found his legs were paralysed and he had to lie there until found the next morning. He had a fractured spine. He died at the 5th Australian General Hospital, Melbourne on the 9th July 1916.

Ernest Poole

Lance corporal 1018 4th Battalion Australian Imperial Force
Date of death: 14/6/1918

Ernest was born in Sydney, New South Wales. He lived at 9 Wetherhill Street, Sydney with his mother Emily. He was a ship deck hand. He enlisted in Liverpool, New South Wales on the 26th November 1914. He was transferred to the Anzac Police Corps on the 3rd April 1916. He died on the 14th June 1918 at the University War Hospital, Southampton, England. He is buried at Hollybrook Cemetery, Southampton.

The circumstances of his death:

He died from paralysis of his lower limbs and acute bronchitis received whilst trying to save a little French child from drowning.

Frank Lyons

Private 3980 7th Field Ambulance
Date of death: 23/3/1916

Frank was born in Liverpool, England. He was a miner. He enlisted on the 7th April 1915. He died on the 23rd March 1916. He is buried at Melun Communal Cemetery, France.

The circumstances of his death:

He died on the 23rd March 1916. He was travelling on the roof of a troop train when his head was in a collision of either a bridge or tunnel. He suffered a fractured skull.

John Henry Ford

Acting corporal   4398   29th Battalion Australian Imperial Force
Date of death: 11/12/1916

John was born in Gatten, Queensland. He enlisted in Narrabri, New South Wales on the 17th March 1916. He was married to Mary. He died on the 11th December 1916.

The circumstances of his death:

He died on board the troop ship HMAT "Afric". He He slipped and fell head first into the ship's canvas bath and broke his spine. He was buried at sea.

Edgar Williams

Private 5482 53rd Battalion Australian Imperial Force
Date of death: 1/7/1916

Edgar was born in Moree, New South Wales in 1896. He enlisted in Goulburn, New South Wales on the 19th November 1915. He embarked at Sydney on the 14th November 1915. He disembarked at Suez. From there he sailed for France, arriving at Marseilles on the 29th June 1916. He died on the 1st July 1916. He is buried at Creil Communal Cemetery, France.

The circumstances of his death:

He was accidentally killed whilst travelling on a troop train from Marseilles, heading to Etaples. Whilst riding on the footboard of the train he was swept off it by some unkown projection on a passing train.

William Edwin Gravell

Private 2856 23rd Battalion Australian Imperial Force
Date of death: 30/6/1916

William was born in Woodend, Victoria in 1887. He lived with his mother Emily at 27 Barrett Street, Albert Park. He enlisted in Melbourne, Victoria on the 3rd August 1915. He died on the 30th June 1916. He is buried at Villers Bretonneux Cemetery, France.

The circumstances of his death:

Whilst travelling on a troop train from Marseilles to Etaples, he fell out of the open window of the carriage door whilst balancing on the seats trying to urinate out of the window, whilst passing La Clayette Station.

John Sullivan

Private 4586 26th Battalion Australian Imperial Force
Date of death: 14/12/1916

John was born in Tipperary, Ireland. He enlisted in Brisbane, Queensland on the 28th December 1915. He died on the 14th December 1916. He is buried at Glanadva Cemetery, Bangor, North Wales.

The circumstances of his death:

He suffered a fractured skull whilst on a train on the 13th December 1916. He died the following day at Bangor Military Hospital.

Witness statement from William James:

I was in charge of the mail train timed to leave Holyhead at 12.22am on Wednesday morning last. Just after passing Bodorgan station the communication cord was pulled. The train was stopped and a soldier was waving out of the window. I went to the compartment and found a soldier badly wounded. He had evidently been struck by something on the head. A Staff Sergeant Hegarty had bandaged the wound. I told the driver to stop at Gaerwen and wire Bangor for an ambulance. There were five other soldiers in the compartment. They said that he was bad in the boat coming over. He put his head out of the window to vomit and fell back badly wounded. His head had come into contact with something.

James Albert Bothwell

Trooper 1316 9th Light Horse
Date of death: 7/8/1917

James was born in Corinella, Victoria in 1891. He enlisted in Melbourne on the 27th July 1915. He died in Moscar, Egypt on the 7th August 1917. He is buried at Ismalia Cemetery, Egypt.

The circumstances of his death:

Witness statement from Lance corporal 805 J Hendry:

" About 6.30am on the 7th August 1917 I came off duty and went to my tent. I laid my belt with revolver on my bed. Trooper Bothwell was there alone. He picked up the loaded revolver, examined it, exclaiming " it appears a good revolver", and put it back after inspection. I left him alone in the tent to go to breakfast. Shortly after sitting down in the mess I heard a shot fired and immediately went out to enquire the cause, and found it was from my tent and that trooper Bothwell was lying on his bunk with a wound in his forehead high up. Splashes of blood were in the tent, high up. He had recently been complaining of pains in his head and eyes."

Printed in Great Britain
by Amazon